ARGUMENTS WITH MORTALITY

HANNIBAL LECTURE

ARGUMENTS WITH MORTALITY

Copyright © 2018 by Hannibal Lecture and Alanna Rusnak Publishing

All rights reserved. This book or any portion thereof may not be reproduced or used in any manner whatsoever without the express written permission of the author except for the use of brief quotations in a book review or scholarly journal.

 First Printing: 2018
ALANNA RUSNAK PUBLISHING

ISBN: 978-0-9959907-3-9
Alanna Rusnak Publishing
282906 Normanby/Bentinck Townline
Durham, Ontario, Canada, N0G 1R0
www.publishing.alannarusnak.com

Contact the publisher for Library and Archives Canada catalogue information.

Cover photography by Hannibal Lecture
Cover design by Alanna Rusnak

Memoratus in Aeternum

Andrew Raymond Chisholm
November 24, 1985 – March 25, 2017

Ronald Patrick O'Day
April 9, 1957 – March 25, 2017

CONTENTS

01 | Zero On Axis
02 | Emery Bored
03 | Poker Face
04 | The Ocean Listens
05 | SIM Cards
06 | Children and Soil
07 | Ground Beef
08 | Zoning Application
09 | Veneer
10 | Burning Journals
11 | Daylight Savings
12 | Simon Says
13 | Marco Polo
14 | Hot Cross Buns
15 | Epitaph
16 | Minesweeper
17 | Speak Without Discipline
18 | Single Stitched
19 | November
20 | The Price of Shampoo
21 | Selfie Stick
22 | CrossFit
23 | Orange Juice & Menthol
24 | Please Don't Mistake It
25 | Airbnb
26 | Mirrors
27 | Scratch and Win
28 | Bismuth
29 | Local Flavour
30 | Scenery
31 | Save the Cat

32 | Qu'est-ce que c'est
33 | Engraving Plates
34 | Full Contact
35 | Sidewalk Gum
36 | Leg Day
37 | To Kill a Mockery
38 | Horticulture
39 | Finger Paint (breathing fabrics)
40 | Clothespins
41 | Sad Notes
42 | Ground Zero
43 | Terms of Service
44 | Tracking Number
45 | Blessings in Sevens
46 | Fireplace Ambiance
47 | Pesto
48 | Expansions Slots
49 | Under Wraps
50 | Game of Loans
51 | Lazy Susan
52 | Fluid
53 | Echoes
54 | Glossolalia
55 | The Barrel

Arguments with Mortality

Hannibal Lecture

2018
Alanna Rusnak Publishing

01 | Zero On Axis

A pulled groin over Long Island's dangerously concave bathtubs
with feet extended six inches past the bow of an enclave mattress,
viewing the Manhattan sunset from the window of a Kennedy Hampton,
exponentially humbled by the sine wave's vastness,
noting the peak deviation of his function from zero on axis
until he registers a notion of the applied mathematics
and the full realization that it's only described cabbage patch kids
and their uniformity regardless of the chosen root gripping landmass.
Paper sails direct the compass to any shore where the sand casts
by way of synthetic ties, plastic tides and ample space to stand back,
or even sit in an attempt to do less grinding of the hand axe
and reflect on the airbus legroom when he only rides last class.
So don't ask him for a postcard without knowledge of the stamp tax
while he gives the twice over to rendered plaques, trying to extract facts.
He kicked it with some disciple statues and stocked up on sumac wax
but the strings fell off the map when he started polishing the brass tacks.

02 | Emery Bored

They hadn't even hurt us yet, so I waited,
chewing a handful of Percocet, dehydrated.
Checking a sundial necklace, like god made it,
for a shadow and a time stamp - I'm that jaded.
Exhausted for keeps, I don't know what's next for me.
Might move out to Arlen to slang some accessories
for clean burning fuels and sources of energy.
Play Pogs with your debit cards and topple the treasury -
got a Zippo for a slammer and a distinct lack of empathy
for your claws in my back and this huge waste of emery.
Bored to the marrow, sick to the stomach, hollow to sensory
perception, and intentionally ignorant to cognitive memories
of a past wealthy in sin and most forms of lechery.
It's growing on me like E. coli - I'm essentially entropy.
Unknown landings when you don't plan your trajectory -
I put my own teeth on the curb and still can't manifest destiny.

03 | Poker Face

Memories of when a high tide once raised all ships
don't quell the waves of a ladle breaking bisque
in a symmetry as sacred as a slipped or compact disc,
so he'll bake a dozen country miles and teach your kittens how to knit
while trying to put a broken finger on exactly what the estate owes,
smelling of blood, sweat and beers - like, "Yo, sedate those."
He has to look it up even though it's right under a straight nose,
so he'll charge his phone with a room full of wiring and potatoes
in a trifecta of isolation, companionship and sacrifice,
like fourteen shots fired over the everlasting ice
of a true northern winter set to no casting rights
or applause, at about forty percent over the asking price
set by the locals after seeing his breath pass through harmonics
in a distinct lack of effort with the leverage to shift tectonics.
Not much more than a broke disgrace who's hooked on tonics,
so excuse him if his poker face has puke on it.

04 | The Ocean Listens

Geneva peace talks on a subject of the lives not living
in the crematorium heat of a Damascus prison
only break bread between those not given
a holy perspective on the horrors they've driven.
Flour, water and time - a fine line between broke and risen
when the slaughterhouse is synonymous with the stolen kitchen
where they bake drone surveillance into a trojan griffin
with no ears to the ground, 'cause only the ocean listens
to the felonious sound of too many lives parishioned
by birth to resource defined sacred jurisdictions
that lay the lines on the maps with a spool of Odin's ribbon
only to blow them away with tools of bespoke ambition.
Remove imperfections from the safety of where the explosion isn't,
securely speaking in silence of their cash woven visions
while turning water to crime. Hope and care won't provoke decisions
of power, fodder and mind. Poke the bear - don't stoke the fission.

05 | SIM Cards

As the bottle spins with cryptic mysticism
and we try to guess to whom the lipstick kiss is given,
he'll snatch and smash it, miss a cyst excision,
half asleep, dead-bored by the characteristic rhythms
of growing up or out, blooming too reckless,
warpaint of clay, wearing a human tooth necklace,
in an age or day when the illusions effect us.
Bulk SIM cards for the click farms, a looming addendum
of wandering too far without leaving the bread crumbs
on a pre-beaten path, by those who just want to get some
little piece of the math and a big hole in their septum
for photos in the bath, in hopes no one forgets 'em.
But he's just as bad - he's got no forward momentum,
nothing to say to most ears they can lend him,
when he opens his mouth, the air's tasting like venom.
Don't look at his feet - he's trying to rest them.

06 | Children and Soil

Label them as ill and destroy their self confidence
at a young enough age that the only shop politics
are what happened in Pallet Town and where Team Rocket is,
because children are the future of where the profit is -
Pfizer knows best for all but the doctor's kids
and parents trust the scribble without feeling lost in it.
Fuel and fund the spinning wheel of incompetence
to see that the arrow points directly to a consequence
of a society of the head sick and their saviour charlatans
who would rather print money than roll nonpartisan.
He's dreaming of an anonymous invite to the conference,
a ski mask, some matches - a jerry can of bottomless
optimism with a flash point that'll stop and drop opulence
along with the collateral under-filled and overpriced colleges.
We poisoned our children and soil - there's no need to contradict
the hard work we'll put into collective unconsciousness.

07 | Ground Beef

Pour smoke in the hive while still losing some ground.
Beef with the butchers and big ups to the down
in every perspective where the foreground is renowned
for wine indentured harlequins - for pissed and poor clowns.
Ain't grasping shit, but still her fist is four pounds.
Something like a role call with no list to pronounce,
so she defaced a good book to twist a whole ounce
over the distaste for the man who fished her mom's accounts.
He put a high premium on something we insist we can't count.
Guess they call it mining because, really - whose is it now?
Dressed like an indecisive loner with a slight procurance habit
to play some tennis with the owner of a life insurance racket,
and get a look at the keypad to cause some violence with a hatchet.
She called it justice, they called it a wild act of madness.
Spent the rest of her days in a tight and backwards jacket,
painting pictures with her eyes, using a ceiling for a canvas.

08 | Zoning Application

Two men down. No, he don't fit the description -
heard four black hoodies on the transmission.
Crew neck, no crew, and a lack of suspicion.
No fire arms, and void of ammunition.
Maybe cop a new fitted, load and lock pistols
until there is little left to quill into acquittals.
Bleed out in a McDonald's and really be belittled -
should've learned from the hippies before slanging brittle crystals.
The fountain of life is a carefully curated tar pit
where the chems will have them surfing dirty carpets
in a high-noon living room, outside the labour market,
that'll never see the sun or make it in the op-ed.
Keep the readers happy and try to keep it topical
in an article as easy to swallow as a popsicle.
Ending gun violence is probably impossible,
but if you zone more cemeteries, you'll need less hospitals.

09 | Veneer

It's the lazy and ignorant, it's the crowdfunded beers.
It's the missing indigenous, it's the highway of tears.
It's the sham they call politics, it's controlling through fear.
It's the violence and wickedness, it's the morales adhered
by voting in confidence without slipping a gear
when the clutch is worn out and the transmission's dear
to the machine, but the wheel won't steer
where we are aiming while all that we hear
are the voices of dead friends from beneath the veneer
we applied to ourselves, trying to coat a career
in the free time we want when the clock is unclear
and the calendar's burning with each passing peer
reduced to a photo where the memories sear
a heart and mind blind, in a pain multi-tiered,
like the one from growing up when they all called you weird,
now seen from a perspective unjaded, sincere.

10 | Burning Journals

She barely has her sea legs when she casts out her lure,
so forgive his nerves when she takes her act on tour.
Some stepped on drugs and intentions less pure,
when land locked drowning is the haute couture.
He'd rather hole up in his shell than jump the hurdles,
meet the Great A'Tuin, drowning cosmic turtles,
'cause the difference between forever and a twisted circle
is indiscernible in verbals gurgled.
Change his last name to Montag and start burning journals
in an attempt to forget or hide what he's left external.
At home he trained to hone his blade, circa dermal,
in case the need imposed to expose the hoax of a life eternal.
Questions of longevity have never been less than fertile
in a hole riddled stomach where the basic curdles.
He'll work on the cage until his chest is purple
in perpetual darkness - learns to fly nocturnal.

11 | Daylight Savings

If he's the Sandy Bridge, y'all nothing more than Nehalem,
watching him play chess against computers until they fucking hate him.
Giving them sentience and some skin to masquerade in
while they give life advice without ever breaking cadence
and adjust their clock speeds for daylight savings,
increase the crime rate. Early nightfall's dangerous
for some of the irate, in a sum of the places
where organic perception only seems to create misshapen racists
who mimic cognitive functions and all run the same playlists
like complacent vacants on their way to Vegas,
or the nameless faces aiming for fame in stasis.
Use natural language processing to learn situational graces
and lure the rest to the Turing test to simulate phrases
while careful what is copied and where the admiration is pasted.
He said, "You must be able to learn, right? Or am I mistaken?"
'I've never really thought about it.' - 'Yeah right, Siri. You're wasted.'

12 | Simon Says

Simon says a lot of things in really busy verbiage
over rice and collared greens while twisting up a tourniquet.
Beta-blocking by all means, but always acting courteous
to the talking arteries - "Yo, where the mortem derby is?"
Twenty-two beats past the closed door on your left -
the one you lost the key for while trying to catch a breath
and break from aging and owning all your debts.
A misplaced bank card can cause a lot of stress
and a piss-tanked hate for a gras dialect.
Now the distaste flanks to prove the cause and effect
of a stomach full of snakes and a broken alphabet.
Shit - we missed the orcus concours while all of that was said.
Might have to make like Fievel, the time he went west
and put these subcelestial vitals to their fucking test.
Like 'obcasus autem nex,' or other clever terms for a son's westward death.
Simon says a lot of things, but no one tells the sun when it sets.

13 | Marco Polo

Apricots discriminating against plums from different orchards
when Monsanto's seeds are the only ovum allowed to cross borders.
So, I smoke through a hole in my throat and get taxed every quarter
on social control methods and gentrified tortures.
I shape tools out of prescriptions when I'm feeling fucking cornered,
and being told that it's less of a distaste and more of a disorder.
Use them and my Alfie Hinds sight to get the fuck out by the morning.
Hit the road and tin foil like there probably ain't tomorrow.
Stumble on a farmhouse in Dunwich and only consume lawyers
until the walls give way to my invisible horrors
and every other brick in the wall is freed from its mortar.
They grow up so fast in a sacrificial order
sworn to secrecy, banned from libraries, and lacking in supporters.
Hot and cold, angry Khan, and a mute Marco Polo
presents a blind man's bluff to trade fur in the former.
When you stop justifying hate, you'll get a little warmer.

14 | Hot Cross Buns

The first breed of hairless apes to harness the power of the sun
and use it for mass murder the moment brunch is done
don't own the responsibility for their tools of fun,
never mind the ones for war. I think it's time we run.
We can't be trusted with a shovel, but yo, here's a fucking gun.
Got all of Mars' rovers, rolling over, one by one -
and every axis line dancing in the cosmic pantheon,
giving crosses to the hungry in lieu of hot cross buns
because we have no daughters and we have no sons.
One a penny, two a penny, it ain't worth his tongue,
so he'll keep it in his cheek and leave every song unsung,
drowsy and inattentive while attempting to appear alert,
he'll hold back the vomit, but prob'ly just until dessert.
For you, himself, and every other thoughtful introvert,
he'll pull down the stars and tell them where the nooses hurt,
wearing an omnidirectional "I'm with fucking stupid" shirt.

15 | Epitaph

If a you go to the gym and no one likes your selfie,
did it really happen? Are you even toned and healthy?
She said creation through observation is the envy
of a culture of ego tender sailing a dead sea
with plenty of fish bobbing belly up to deadbeats.
That very moment, I swallowed the hotel key,
presenting a bouquet of a gorgeous dead three
blind mice looking at you like they really can see
through your laws of protection like a vigilante
who really loves palm trees and will never see Miami.
This has been my least favourite daily trip to hell and back,
so I'll make a stick and poke scratcher on my belly laugh,
stating that my best homie Ben will prob'ly write my epitaph
and take over my unfinished business, like, "Yo, it's a wrap."
Because I know that he too will always have the sense to smell a rat
while discerning whether it's an overbearing camera flash, snake or staff.

16 | Minesweeper

He don't own a voice box or an illogical timekeeper,
but he do own a robot who's really good at minesweeper
and curtain calling the crude organic life theatre.
Admission was high and he wasn't feeling the playwright either.
Grows tired of spanning the gaps between the spaced out feeders
and tending to the reel as they leave it to beaver,
so he gets hired relapsing, relaxing - jeans and no sneakers.
The firewater irony walker feels his soles weaken
on his way to the flat taxing two litre beacon.
Cursing through the cough at his two breathers beaten
down to the rocks by the flats that be leaving him bleeding.
Might need a six pack and laugh track - ain't leaving here breathing.
Checking the timelines and road maps - shit's crumpled, can't read 'em.
Planned to look back and wiretap this most needless of seasons.
Mark his route sidetracked and hijacked by two needles of treason.
Found a toe tag and flatline without the achievement of reason.

17 | Speak Without Discipline

I told them to share the apple, 'cause they no longer grow on trees.
One said, "You're an asshole, I'ma take your leg at the knee."
To which I replied, "Bruh, it ain't worth the disease."
The other didn't look hungry in a toupee of maltese
and I couldn't understand his words through the wheeze
and foreign dialect, I think Cantonese.
Thought it odd for a farm animal wearing blue on the beat,
so I put 'em both on the spit and tighten the ropes at their feet.
The hereafter is strange and I find it interesting
how it's designed for bipeds with aversive conditioning.
Time to move to the dark net so I can speak without discipline
and use quantum cryptography to tell if they're listening,
check the state of my photons and note frequency dissonance,
spoof a physical address and hide where the wicked is.
The imprisonment of information is imminent,
so eat the anthrax and be convinced it's cinnamon.

18 | Single Stitched

Whether a self cannibalistic manicure for your nerves and appearance
or some anachronistic traffickers for these nerds' perseverance,
it'll get there in due time, regardless of the kinship or coherence
imperative to bio-mechanical massacres and their compulsory remittance
paid in full, up front, by those who are undeniably on clearance
and slacking by way of forthcoming terms of service and endearment.
They say it only gets better, and maybe one day he'll believe it
when every sentence doesn't end with a period of bereavement.
Oh, the things he'd trade for a barren diner, or an airtight bare sign of
what he dislike more, the air in China, or the airline - Air China.
They made him turn off his devices, or he would've tried to write a
dissertation on the comeback of analog by way of vinyl
on the precipice of learning chipsets, hoping it might define the
boiling point of his marrow, or the taste of blood in his saliva.
His whole life is single stitched, and he's blaming the designer
who left his seams splitting somewhere between messiah and pariah.

19 | November

It was an unseasonably warm start to November,
he puked more times than he could hope to remember
or forget. It's all perspective quilled in the head of a letter
addressed to the dead and other birds of a feather.
So he broke his finger with a hammer, without losing his temper,
over a knee that still kills from weeks ago, when he caught a fender
that tore his MCL and put his attitude through the blender.
Didn't miss much work, in an effort to get that legal tender -
he's been using his other hand to pull the punch card lever.
I guess it can never be a home run when the ball's on a tether
and the fabrication department forgot to stitch the leather.
Found some inspiration in the recycled words of Brooks Decker
and penned a few poems in the alley behind the community centre
while trying to avoid writing them all about the unusual weather.
Halfway through a thirty day stasis that'll prob'ly last forever -
he never thought he'd say it, but he can't wait until December.

20 | The Price of Shampoo

An eye mask for beauty sleep and hate of the view,
it seems like every new city has a Park Avenue -
she can't get what she wants and not have it too,
while finding a new address, but just passing through.
Continues a cycle of the tried and not true,
wondering why every trip to the links is mulligan stew,
and asking who built the walls she keeps bumping into,
why all the wrong things are in judicial review,
and drying her tears in leathered pleura tissue.
Less credit to organs, more to the latest misuse
of starting fluid ether to clean airways of glue,
only to start choking on the price of shampoo,
looking in the mirror, adjusting a bill overdue.
It's about the coverup, it's nothing to do with hue.
Even when roses are red, and violets are blue,
we act in self preservation, that ain't nothing new.

21 | Selfie Stick

There's a chance that if he could ever stop snoring,
he'd take the opportunity to quill a short story
of regret for the moment he took that WD-40
to his self installed nightingale flooring -
an open invite for the assassins and the boring
with no discernible address underscoring
tour dates promoted through a loop back recording
of armchair activists as they selfie stick it to the man
in an effect that provokes him to lick a bloody hand -
dress a few wounds as to keep doing what he can
to keep two feet grounded on over cultivated land,
trying his damnedest not to isolate a grand,
finance his own hit and put you on the alert,
sweeping the backyard on a trail of stitches and hurt
until you find him tuckered under eight inches of dirt,
kicking buckets, comfy, in the grave he deserves.

22 | CrossFit

I leave shots of bleach on the counter at parties,
wearing a staple gun for brass knuckles and hardly
flinching at the prospect of stealing your car keys
and loading up your entourage on my way to part seas.
Harvesting the organs of CrossFit as fuck sociopaths,
rarely fucking up the carpet - I do it mostly in baths.
You never shit where you eat but where I'm posted I stash
a kidney cooler for an ottoman while I'm smokin' the hash.
I show up to work with Wednesday eyes and lens correction,
looking forward to the weekend in both directions.
Got wounds on the inner walls of my midsection
that don't seem to hurt as bad when amidst connection,
so I always make time for a little Miss Understanding.
And even though this poetry shit can be demanding,
I've never rolled an ankle halfway through rebranding -
that's probably why they say I always stick the landing.

23 | Orange Juice & Menthol

Flipping a coin displaying the two faces of a sick day and no-show,
with self employment at the end of an infinite rainbow.
He'll head to the woods looking for a patsy or scapegoat
for the negative space that populates his bankroll
while Sukhi Barber teaches him that it's about balance and equals.
He takes exactly what he's learned to the frequently feeble,
while they pour slowly through the doors of a deceitful cathedral,
and invokes the ancient flame of a penal upheaval
in the souls of the beings unaware that they're people with free will.
Then he'll wax the floors with philosophy stating that it doesn't have to be a bleak world
and that maybe our next chapter can just be a peaceful sequel.
This all might be too much to ask for, now that we've made free speech illegal,
so he'll take an eraser to every little thing penned in pencil,
along with the colony to the south's president's credentials -
shine light on the dim view and burn the judgemental
while praising the curative properties of orange juice and menthol.

24 | Please Don't Mistake It

He gains his credibility from having weird hair,
and wearing high hats got him trapped in a snare
like a common vermin straight wrapping a pair
of barbed bracelets to his ankles as he yearns to prepare
for a homecoming ushered in by certain despair.
Got a couple stops on the way to get his ground covered -
didn't know one'd fuck him like no other.
Half court perspective that don't even beat the buzzer
as a he drops a dap and hug for his dead friend's brother.
Now he's gotta stop and enjoy some art he doesn't understand.
The boy's no spring chicken, he's a dozen summer hams
found in a dumpster by an inked lover's covered hands,
or maybe a mute rooster with some 'wake up' knuckle tatts.
Ain't gonna happen to that little sleepy lame kid.
One lid's always open with an eye on his blanket,
and he only bring bad news, so please don't mistake it -
he only got tattoos so he can look cool naked.

25 | Airbnb

It was terribly unnerving because he spoke the same language
as the cauldron operators who he didn't want to hang with
regardless of the freezing needle or a promise that it's painless,
like the pre-bill chatter forced by your favourite waitress,
but he's the one plunging when it was their shit that clogged the porcelain.
They left the fan on and bounced in hopes they'd find their origin
while riding on his back, picking off the pieces of his dorsal fin
and looking for an empty box to hide that jigsaw morsel in.
All the thumb tacks and cut corners were once a brilliant hobby,
now reduced to a habit as useful as a missing car key,
so quote him when he says, "Get this instance off me
and give a guy a minute to ice his instant coffee."
English breakfast where only the continental drift remains
and the eleventh course taught us how the fucking rich complain.
Long weekend incoming - just an elaborate invite to pissing paint,
but it's probably worth it - the Airbnb's fitted with wrist restraints.

26 | Mirrors

If you're having trouble mastering your surrounding social politics,
let him tell you that neither Myers or Briggs were ever a psychologist
and type testing is as binary as full metal jackets versus hollow tips.
Though, they say the heavens leave the softest sunlight over scarlet lips,
because the clouds are better gods than solid states or spinning discs.
I wouldn't trust a rain forest and blood sniffing ideologist
who's prob'ly heard of elf on a shelf - they're going to hate a Hannibal
on an alchemical mixture of unthinkable parallels
born of theoretical metrical through an ethical reticle
focused on several debtor qualms, including a better all.
"Oh, that's such a shame." No, it isn't, you volunteered
for making all the pains disappear with an elaborate system of mirrors
until the public applauds, congratulates you and your peers
on a job not done. But, the importance lies in how it appears,
whether they're on-, or in line, or already at the cashier,
it's all in a day. They never left home, but love the frontier.

27 | Scratch and Win

Pissing into cups and giving away his blood,
using sound to see his insides, then he hit the club,
just trying to get his kidneys stoned and never sober up,
while observing in the third to quell a lonely love.
Makes a bed and lies in it, in a DIY catacomb
fashioned from a wrath of thought that won't leave him alone.
Wonders if they'll ever want to let him back home
smelling so strongly of campfire and goat blood cologne.
So he gets Schrödinger's cat to cash his scratch and win tickets
with his eyes closed to every white fence that you picket,
contemplating the necessity of having a hat fitted,
over the company of a night sky and some chirping crickets.
He'll take this chance to misquote something scholarly
while opening lock boxes where only the passing time is key,
'cause signs about trespass never meant a lot to he,
or the wayward PokeMasters all up on your property.

28 | Bismuth

Judging functionality by the condition of the door frames
while denouncing all the broken systems from which the poor came,
and touching up his makeup before peaking out the storm drain.
Tie up the chimera and keep him on a short rein
with a sharp bit, tack up with blinders - normal marrow's free,
yet they're still all asleep beneath the borrachero tree.
Warbling through the swamp, disturbing the water sparrow's reeds,
while trying to plead their case before the lonely pharaoh's feet.
So, he buys a hat with crooked math, he doesn't really own his own.
He tells his cat he'll be right back, he doesn't really need a smoke.
Exclaiming facts, he won't turn back - light it up the whole way home.
Shaking habits, they're shaking ass - a dog without a bone to throw.
Nonetheless, he might disarm the warheads and cop a citrus grimace,
spit them out and ponder if the effort's worth his business,
weighed against the push pins he's been harbouring since Christmas,
either way he'd like you to stay the fuck out his bismuth.

29 | Local Flavour

You should probably talk to him about what were rumours
in five years when robots have replaced all the fast food workers
because your labor secretary is the CEO of Carl's Jr
and Hardee's - a face for a generation of android boomers
who shouldn't have bitten the apple and gotten lost in the sewers
before they ran out of golems to build for the consumer
inside themselves, over the divine humour of a benign tumour
when the wine steward should've died sooner.
Probably could've been saved if it didn't vanish in malpractice
when every one of your favourite cities went the way of Atlantis
and all that mattered for a week in time was an uninspired rap diss
that would've held less weight if you were better at semantics and mad libs.
That said, he's trying to keep his bubble free and avoid the space invaders,
but he's just a fully grown and misguided mischief maker
who got some cash for the holidays and called it litmus paper -
used it to check the PH balance of his guts against the local flavour.

30 | Scenery

Burnt the back skin - cracked the screen, tallying diverse modalities,
though if you ask him, he's never been that much of a personality,
but he's become pretty decent at penning a verse and rallying
the disasters, the love, the corpses tossed clear from the balcony,
the rain, and the tragedies found in this modern day alchemy.
They stood on his neck and pulled his feet until he was free from the shell
and they never heard a peep - the skin was nothing more than a prison and a hell
gripping wings - long clipped, his first attempt to fly is when he fell
into an abyss of repetitious scenery seen from a limping carousel
of mythical rarities all hailing from the same fucking shelf.
But he don't want to be the one to tell them as they lose all sense of self
worth and individuality as they curl ten digits, trying to count to twelve.
Like when they couldn't have a toy because eating was more important
and they thought it was tough love but really mom couldn't afford it,
or maybe they've never been hungry or learned too young what divorce is.
Either way, we learn to play - experiences are rarely choices.

31 | Save the Cat

Looking for a different kind of answer than the one that booked my hand
for the crown council's marionette control bar of another man
who's probably not sound of mind enough to stand trial or recant
for actions he likely doesn't remember or even understand.
Just a little knife wielding arson that doesn't seem like it was planned -
I probably wouldn't have stopped it if I didn't want to save the cat.
Really, after he pulled the knife he should've made the dash,
he can't expect to light a fire, hang out and get a pass -
people live upstairs, dying ain't in the forecast.
I wouldn't put money on the help he needs - he's probably getting stashed
in a tiny concrete room with nothing but time to think about his past.
I'll smoke one for that lunatic the day his cell door slams
and hope that next time he torches something it's their witness stand,
while I thank idolatries for guilty pleas and fire the summons in the trash.
I ain't a cop or a firefighter and I ain't got time to reprimand
or fight a different kind of cancer than the one that took my aunt.

32 | Qu'est-ce que c'est

Set to task, whiskey sick, in a french café
when they ask what it is, like 'qu'est-ce que c'est?'
Tells 'em he's got a lot more to burrow and a lot less to say
since all his tomorrows became yesterdays.
But if he felt like talking, he'd prob'ly trade
a few short sighted comments about wasted days,
followed by a rehashed perspective on what defines 'okay'
and an extensive report on why it ain't worth the pain.
She might want him back, but a few things have changed
now that he's seen more death than a rifle in the fray.
His teeth are all busted, his toothpaste is gravel.
Hands bloodied by barbed-wire, but shoes laced for battle.
Using kid gloves to kill a snake for its rattle
and remove a few arrows from a face lifting apples.
To all the glory made from quarrel and waters a bit less travelled,
not every story needs a moral, not every boat needs a paddle.

33 | Engraving Plates

Moonlight on fallen birch contrasted by the flickering flame
of a well-nigh empty bic, held arm's length out of frame,
sets the mood and vibe for a folktale fable explained
through the transient humility of human joy and pain.
It goes, "Most people stop nibbling when they taste the blade,
but for some misery and comfort are just two shades of grey
that can't be distinguished in such a hazy place
that don't like maps, and gets off on erasing faiths.
Did I mention you have to work for food? Mostly engraving plates
fashioned from recycled shackles and old daisy chains."
So, shoot him a text if you want to disagree in the rain,
or write your own short story about a wounded beast in a cave
with no ceiling and several occult sigils engraved
to the walls they've padded over concerns and claims
about the safety of himself and others, or the way he behaves.
Either way, he'll be waiting for that text with both legs in the grave.

34 | Full Contact

This night hag ain't the only thing we're trying to get off our chests
while writing it all down in a sans serif ouija typeset.
The silver linings have been burnt, crumpled, and set to fucking rest
with all the trash worth hiding from those who care enough to check
in on the self induced loneliness of the horribly depressed.
The king's pawn opening outdated when the bishop cashed the cheque -
Kasparov isn't the only one who's good at playing chess.
Cap and gown ceremonies to kick start years of hopeless debt
with two strokes and poorly mixed fuel to vignette your sunsets.
I'm just here, trying to jump rope for heart, at odds with the ends
of a wax coated hurdle passing by in the tens
of thousands of things I'll probably never comprehend.
Something to be said for living life through a full contact lens
with flags on my belt in case culture's looking to make amends.
While y'all worry about potentially rolling in a Benz,
I'm watching fentanyl kill all of my favourite friends.

35 | Sidewalk Gum

Wet cement hand prints in an effort to ignore that we're futureless
while counting blessings in fractions until they start to seem numerous,
and dropping characters from formulas while filling the pews at funerals.
All black everything, and some daps from the Lutherans
keep the knuckles hard and the tongue sharp, but dubious.
Emergency oxygen systems demoed by the stewardess
in a fall of bids elating the baddest in what's new to us,
while all the kids updating their status from the uterus
in a step to inundate the cabbage patch eucharist,
start to look evermore like some lost and tragic tourists
giving the old college try to put some magic in their school bus.
That being said, it's hard to look both ways on the bends,
bare knee in sidewalk gum, both hands on our heads.
So we redesign the planet to fit our needs, and invest
in something more valuable than the stock worth our two cents.
Or maybe we'll just lay down. We're tired, and this has been a lot to digest.

36 | Leg Day

A snow globe that's more like a room full of moths,
inverted stairs, a beach, and several melting clocks.
Trying to find proper pacing in an ever plodding plot
in a perpetual leg day, running from problems taught
by the guild coffer who's pocketing a prophet. Not
to be confused with an absconded oracle in promise bought
for three shy of a baker's dozen and twice the discount sought
by the billed poppers destitute in all but impounded thought,
using mace for body spray in an abandoned parking lot
and putting random access memory over a troubled expansion slot.
Sailing on a garbage fashioned raft with the winds at a tablecloth,
forcing the voyage shore bound to the banks laden in ocelot
eyes, illuminating a seaboard of your children's booster shots,
about eighteen fathoms over an out of work aquanaut
who's long lost his guide line and never the learnt the windsor knot.
He might turn up, facedown in high water, in a partitioned melting pot.

37 | To Kill a Mockery

They'll write you shitty quotes just to get you undressed,
make a couple bucks off your teenage distress
while some asshole named Sylvester McNutts on your chest
and j. butter word somehow thinks he's the best.
And while I do believe this dude is high as fuck,
don't talk to me about a poet's society if you fucking suck
the tits of the dead. It's called plagiarism, bruh -
Nothing to do with writing or, for that matter, luck.
I'll Discover Poetry with the front end of a truck
and take back an art form from those who sapped it into pallidness
and killed and mocked the important name of Atticus,
put it on the grill and baste it like a rack of ribs,
only to shit it out in a blatant display of callousness.
Robber M. Drake will take what he takes,
put his name under it and run with the snakes.
R.H. a sin of the 'chaos within' - you're all fucking fakes.

38 | Horticulture

In a haunted, hazy living room, getting underused eyelids tattooed
to the distracting harmony of being lied to over Thai food,
pondering the parallels between a carousel and monsoon
constructed wholly by the usual afternoon of salt wounds.
Their adult braces are too tight to fit any truth between the teeth.
All the best conversations are had with the ghosts from far beneath
the soil of life conversion - baby, carbon date a swordless sheath
counted by the fourth, the eighth, the sixteenth, and breathe.
Stop the misdirection for long enough to spot the intersection
of a missed detention crossing lonely paths with a rhythm section
sampling only a sad horn orchestra's imperfections -
the sound of insanity's immaculate in conception.
Do it once - a distaste for the upshot. Funny what we condemn
in the months with the cold air and gut rot, remembering those times we dreamt.
It could very well be the blood, or maybe it's the phlegm -
the consequences are the flowers, the choices are the stems.

39 | Finger Paint

Lipstick mashed into a sheetless mattress
in a garden of broken bones and breathing fabrics,
checkered by the grid of a leaning lattice
and the soft distant glow of a grieving actress,
can be found if you look close at the hidden axis
of a half charted map in a heathen's atlas.
Find him two pages over, completing blacklists
of those who'll never know, and he won't let practice.
A good place to relax with a healing chalice
embellished with the stories of a screaming madness,
and topped to the rim with genealogy extracted
from the nigh heeded advice of a bleeding baptist,
while auditing spreadsheets of well meaning past sins
on his way past the spines of a teething cactus.
The only way to disembowel these means on canvas
is seppuku before he's prey to the feeding mantis.

40 | Clothespins

Reaching with your teeth and dreams wrapped up in moleskin
on your way to pull down the night sky with no limbs.
The one with the step ladder prob'ly has the most wins
when all your cosmos are hung up by clothespins.
A stretch you'll take on the chin with a shield of bathtub gin
in a tailspin of banana skin over the mandolin you once dabbled in.
Find someone who can tell me why, in all of this,
there simply aren't more female gynaecologists,
and why a nation's pastime is mostly just hit or miss.
Might be all balls, but you ain't walking less you hit a pitch
off the plate, playing through the pain of a shoddy wrist.
Jump through the pretzeled hoops and watch the way your body twists
to a shape with which your mind declines to coexist.
That being said, I steeple my fingers that y'all get the gist
of not much more than a maze or a partial list.
It's all fucking broken - even Isaac Hayes' a Scientologist.

41 | Sad Notes

He fell asleep in Sodom, he woke up in Gomorrah.
He sells leaves to autumn, he sells north to aurora
borealis, and won't be caught dead in a fedora.
Stores his malice - it'll be boxed, ready for Pandora
when she gets bored of reflecting her Mac and Sephora,
or grows done with trying to hold a flame to his aura.
Kidding, it's lens flare - and he thinks her name was Laura.
It gets hard to articulate when his memories are foreign
and all but his right foot left the box right before a
series of unwound and broken clocks made of coral
sang stories of the all gifted, all giving, as if it were normal.
Pithos or pathos, a box or sad notes, it's all in quarrel
of the curiosity that neither god nor man called amoral
when she let him out the jar at the expense of mortals,
so excuse him for a minute while he explores a
place to lie down, somewhere among the flora.

42 | Ground Zero

Stuck in an interesting and uncomfortable dichotomy
of, 'If I follow you, would you maybe follow me?'
Whether using your location data to map out your geography
or your hashtags and history to pinpoint your idolatries,
it all boils down to gaining a monopoly on monotony
while employing a theology of technology responsibly.
Found some solace in the day he lost his phone and his visa
until they were dowsed by the witch sticks of a shoeless girl named Paprika,
who swore up and down that she couldn't see through the amnesia
and that every morning felt like ground zero Hiroshima.
In an age where it's hard to find some paper to roll his weed up,
it's a damn good thing he just got slapped with a subpoena.
Burns it back and says goodbye to the summons,
along with the moral cage and the pains in his stomach -
breaking through the fourth wall and hunting
for some insight through stitched eyes of black buttons.

43 | Terms of Service

Probably far better off sleeping with sea anemones
than waking everyday to an intake of CNNemies.
All hope isn't lost. We can see a few remedies
in freedom imbedded in technology's tenancies.
When the NSA issues a new decree of felonies
and tries to keep it checked, along with our l-m-n-o-p's,
we keep it out of sequence and blanket it with an element of keys
so the monitor of all communications can't perceive what it reads.
We're all fucking criminals, but only some of us are chosen
to be examples when your little terms of service end up broken.
Rest in peace Aaron Swartz, and live in peace Edward Snowden.
Shoutouts to everyone else who's paying more than they're owing.
When intelligent civil disobedience hits congress
they'll have to do a little more than wait-list the watch-list.
We're millions strong and can't stop putting nails in your coffins.
We are anonymous and we keep our names out your log-ins.

44 | Tracking Number

Writing tracks about turning tracks up louder
while I burn back a bit of that Lil Debbie downer,
then ponder the irony of what a trap movement empowers
with my feet up, waterboarding myself in the shower.
Might seem like fun, but it lost its charm in an hour
measured by a tick-tocking clock, face caked in white powder,
next to Dick Dawkins' watch laid to waste on the counter,
accompanied by some Ray Charles shades and fold-up hammer
of red and white - either a courtesy to others or a symbol of valor.
None of which would carry much importance in answer
if you're still left with questions about the bedside manner
of a wooden horse brimming with phantom cadavers,
already CAT Scanned for all forms of bad cancers,
some whack rap stances, and stanza advancements.
Didn't find the latter, they must still be in transit
with my ransom note. It reads, "Just send a casket."

45 | Blessings in Sevens

Making blackout poems out of civil rights documents
as he recycles the words with intent to follow them
until they land as litter on the steps of parliament,
privy to the command economy, or whatever they're calling it.
Or he'll obtain a blood meal while avoiding host acknowledgment
so he can spend another winter in diapause - delay most development.
Vasectomy's arcane in appeal while toiling, coaxed, appalled in lent -
forty-six past Ash Wednesday, just trying to get dosed and then repent
a way through the hunger. Lift a book, get close - don't raise the dead.
He knows they don't eat meat on a Fridays, and that they're having fish instead
but, the line's tangled around his ankles and the water's at his neck.
No fear of your tide, though - he's been conditioned to hold his breath
while fishing for some solitude. It's never felt like less a threat
on an Easter Sunday, probably better spent in bed,
staring to the heavens, stifling the hell that's in his head,
counting blessings in sevens, with no ceiling on his tent.

46 | Fireplace Ambience

Most of Santa's elves are underpaid children in third world countries
working around the clock just to go home hungry
in the advent of a nativity fast that starts to get ugly
when the feast of the twelfth night doesn't hit their tummies
ever. I wonder why St. Nick's colour way is that of an ambulance
and start to question if I'm splitting hairs or if it was an accident
that the Netherlands display their elves in such callousness.
There seems to be division in the unified festal cycle - it's passionless.
Round twenty-eight and wondering if I can still handle this
whirlwind of disharmony illuminated by fireplace ambience
in an old pagan celebration of winter solstice through crapulence
on its way to so much more with mistletoe, lights and extravagance.
Or maybe I'll chill. Got gifts, decor and a magical cloud man who loves me
regardless of what I fuel with my allotted time and money.
Let's get that holiday nog and some tinsel, let's get comfy
while you peep my new MacBook. Ain't the first world lovely?

47 | Pesto

Shoes off, bug bites, smoking - al fresco,
swallow all the fireflies, curating a dead zone
necessary for penning a poppy seed yes-no
version of a lost in deep dream manifesto
on a sleeping pill subjective to a basement burlesque show,
acting like a poet whilst breaking the dress code.
He don't like your band, and no, it's not because of the tempo,
it's more the lyrical content lifted straight from The Pet Goat,
set to rest upon the bread like self spreading pesto
shadowed by an olive branch growing pimento
of its own, after altering its genealogy
in attempts to overgrow every farm across the colony.
Sell a Slinky to Escher, try to fulfil another prophecy
of lobotomy without a need for an apology -
disparate events often culminate in cacophony
so fucking audible it could topple the autonomy.

48 | Expansion Slots

When you get the shower temperature ideal right off the hop,
then feel the need to change it, acclimated or not.
Yeah, kind of like that, but more like a one shot,
an indoor gunshot. Ears ringing and whatnot.
So he tied surgeon's knots over his expansion slots
to protect his kilowatts from the booster shots
and his food for thought from the juggernaut,
knowing that life alert will be an app by the time that he needs it,
soon to be freed from the mortal coil and the way that he sees it.
He's packing a gas mask in his carry-on for various reasons,
mostly for pollution and nefarious treason,
only after he attends to a few things while change is in season.
Really just his shirt, though. Got a new job - seems decent.
Sit back and watch the idea depletion while still believing
in some coffee or an apple for the sleepy legions
over the taste of irony, he knows he's dreaming.

49 | Under Wraps

It can all be found in the simple intrinsic riddles
while holding exclusive lighter flame lit illicit vigils.
The code'll be hidden in plain sight, in specific pixels
and the coordinates'll be sent through encrypted sigils
in a visage that leaves all but the humble vexed and confused,
like a dude's face that's covered with acne and tattoos,
displayed on strange paper photos that don't illuminate rooms
or require a password or biometrics to numerate views.
They fermented and bottled every last grape of wrath
for the soul purpose of keeping disposition under wraps.
It's about giving in, it's never been about giving back -
those are the moments put out to pasture with the days of tact.
A collective unknowing that never learned to love
the two sides of the coin, a tax increase or a service cut.
Maybe just pocket the coin through a dispersal of poisoned drugs,
then wait for the dust to settle - wipe your hands of the servant's blood.

50 | Game of Loans

Sitting on a bird stopper that's less of a pain in the ass
than needing to eat in a culture that's solely based on class.
Economics can be fun if you're the one who gets the cash
and a life to live in comfort rung from the sweat pushed from their backs
into tattered t-shirts, or whatever you've let them have.
I see you have a fair trade lampshade. So, yeah - don't feel so bad;
it's only the lives of millions that makes yours so fucking rad.
Ignorance is bliss - that's probably why, in fact,
that a trinity sewn analyst tries less to understand
the clinically stoned callousness and broken, skinny hands
of a cynically cloned masochist coasting in to plan
an intrinsically owned abacus to boast a click or clack.
Set to pilfer the unknown - launch sailboats to seas of trash.
He'll get lifted taking loans and make the most of eating glass
while sullen, shaping bones to make a toast to how he acts
like that kid from Game of Thrones who's like The Ghost of Christmas Past.

51 | Lazy Susan

Let him work on re-centring his convenience
for the assholes and demons who'll prob'ly never feel this
while they mistake his patience for a weakness,
like the sound it makes when we ping-pong the swan song
somewhere between headstrong and stepped on,
hoping never to find himself in the same hurry,
when they tell him, "Don't defame the blameworthy."
Like it'll make their parlour game a safe journey
to the shocking development of a foregone conclusion
drawn by a podiatrist with foot fetish, spinning a lazy susan
into Archimedean spirals of long-sought optical illusions
of a pipe dream overdose guised as hemoglobin transfusion.
While the families ran from wildfires to find solace in air pollution,
he wrote a story about the birds and the origin of humans,
their inevitable demise and the clean slates of evolution.
The public reading was less of a revolt and more of an execution.

52 | Fluid

The story has some twists, but we're still not sure what the premise is
when the purification scrub refused to remove the blemishes,
only causing more and putting some Stockholm in the genesis
of something far more important than the next round of beverages.
While the beads slide on the abacus, counting calendar days,
wrought with self destruction in the least violent of ways -
we're trying to think of clever quips just to title the waves
breaking against the shorelines of shallow, idle-dug graves,
in an inspiring rhythm that makes the primal engage -
fighting house fires with gasoline, falling asleep in the blaze.
Wake to the ashes, blinders on - reassign the threonine,
intake the rations with grace, only crying wine from time to time.
Won't ever question the pace of a fragile mind in slow decline
with no co-pilot yoke to make the lack of climb more benign,
considering the basics of food, fluid, fun and reproduction,
too quick to forget that the fun fluids run with repercussions.

53 | Echoes

We often find it difficult, keeping calmness in our bonnets -
as a whole, we usually toss it at the farthest
from where it'll stick, and act surprised by the losses
when it comes time to engage in the charmless harvest
that we learnt from dream journals in a heartless harness
that only seems to chafe. The size-chart was dishonest.
The modus operandi is lending partial hardships,
unearthed by the grasp of a walking carcass,
to the severed ears of all the target markets.
It doesn't take much practice to pen a dark catharsis -
it's as easy as walking or breathing, or confusing art with artist.
Even the good dreams are nettled by a sordid mollusk
and a looped .wav file of an ever dripping faucet.
Looked at how he found it, and that's the way he lost it,
so he records it all in the echoes of haunted closets
in hopes you will listen when he finally stops his talking.

54 | Glossolalia

The vitamins don't work if they don't make your piss stink,
and there's mint in the face scrub in hopes to make you think
that it's even working when the tingle makes your eyes blink
to the millions who also pine to make their pores shrink.
Chomping at the bit to make euphemisms about horses -
put down for a lame foot, losing time where his voice is.
The local towels lack absorbency - he would probably just forfeit,
but his away game is incredible. Fact check it with your sources
who only sleep on Thursdays. Everyday's a fucking Friday
with the durability of a soap bubble, blown by the almighty,
towards a pin board in the tropical winds of Hawaii,
used to display the clutter that most consider unsightly.
Wire toothbrush to scrub from his mouth that flavour of blood,
knowing full well he won't be paid for a labour of love.
From what he could tell, they were hating in tongues.
Two months later, still hacking Beijing from his lungs.

55 | The Barrel

To make it beautiful, sometimes parts need to be trimmed off,
but it's up to us where we pour our sawdust of scrimshaw -
whether we land in a polarity of disgust for limb loss
or touch down in a dichotomy of distrust and grim thoughts.
Seems like almost everyone is getting sick of pissing out pre-cum
over every lipstick written napkin note that reads "please run."
Red eyes over fresh breath, eye deep in marine mud,
trying to discern between a menthol or Listerine mean mug
while picking out the seeds and stem cells at the foot of a low mountain
range with three burners, as profound and
as exciting as LEDs behind a waterless fountain.
For a few dollars more it comes with a side of bottomless counting,
looking at clocks as though the time only breeds flaws,
trying to let go of it all while erasing every line that we saw,
with a soviet spinning wheel that'll rub our psyches raw
from the chamber of a mirror, down the barrel of a straw.

The Poet | Hannibal Lecture

Hannibal is a prolific and fast-rising young, Canadian poet. He cut his teeth writing and reading for those late-night/early-morning, pill-popping drunks who hung around his old pad - but has since found a larger audience, taking his writing online. In so doing, Hannibal has come to the attention of thousands of new fans - including acclaimed, printed publications; and has even drawn the eye of several of his own musical and literary heroes. Drawing inspiration from real life - whether it be those rare and covetous joyous moments, the absurdities of inane convention, or the harrowing ordeals that plague the human condition - Lecture speaks to all these, and is thus a renewing force; bringing interest and credibility back to a noble medium, now seemingly relegated to haunted, dusty old shelves of stale libraries. In spite of his success and ascent through the highly competitive, dime-a-dozen, Thunderdome of professional writing, this young poet from British Columbia retains a strong sense of humility and self-awareness, evident in his prose - in poems that speak directly to the readers, no matter whom; for Hannibal Lecture is a poet of the streets, inspired by those people he observes there.

www.ingramcontent.com/pod-product-compliance
Lightning Source LLC
Chambersburg PA
CBHW060219050426
42446CB00013B/3109